TELL ME WHY

The Molecules That Make You YOU

ROBERT E. WELLS

illustrated by

PATRICK CORRIGAN

Albert Whitman & Company
Chicago, Illinois

For Allegra, Jon, Everett, and Cleia—
each truly unique, yet more than 99% the same—REW

For my brother James—PC

Library of Congress Cataloging-in-Publication data is on file with the publisher.
Text copyright © 2022 by Robert E. Wells
Illustrations copyright © 2022 by Albert Whitman & Company
Illustrations by Patrick Corrigan
First published in the United States of America in 2022 by Albert Whitman & Company
ISBN 978-0-8075-7774-5 (hardcover) • ISBN 978-0-8075-7775-2 (ebook)
Printed in China
10 9 8 7 6 5 4 3 2 1 WKT 26 25 24 23 22
Design by Aphelandra
For more information about Albert Whitman & Company, visit our website at www.albertwhitman.com.

Our world is full of living things. Some fly in the air or swim in the water. Some are born, and some are hatched. Many of them grow from seeds in the ground. But no matter their sizes or shapes, all living things are made of cells.

You are a living thing, so you are made of cells. Cells are the smallest living structures that can function by themselves. They are so tiny you need a microscope to see them. Your body is made up of trillions of them!

Your cells are very similar to the cells in a cat or a fish or a bird. So is it just by chance that you were born a human being?

human cell

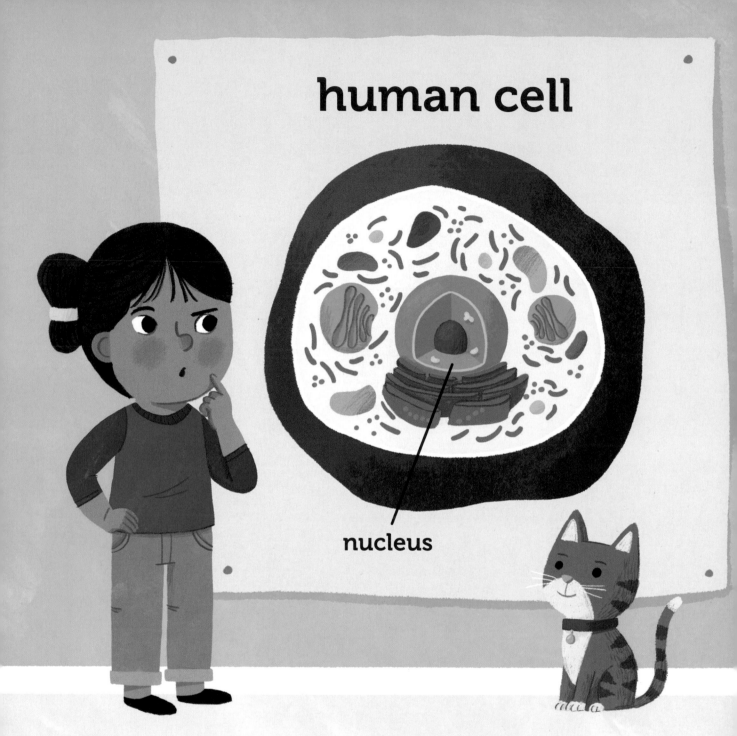

nucleus

Certainly not! A human cell has many tiny parts inside.
It's controlled by a round center called a nucleus.
Within the nucleus are molecules that contain the
plans to make you a person. They are called DNA
molecules, and they're part of what makes you you.

DNA molecule

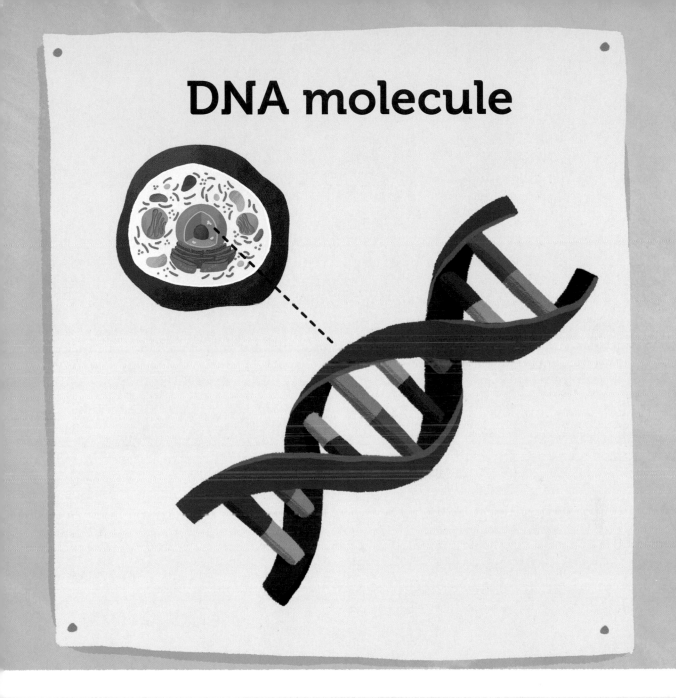

The letters *DNA* stand for a tongue-twisting pair of words: *deoxyribonucleic acid*. These words are pronounced *dee-ahk-see-rye-bow-new-clay-ick as-id.* "Deoxyribonucleic acid" is fun to say, but "DNA" is much faster.

DNA molecules are thousands of times thinner than a cat's whisker, and very long. If all the DNA in just one of your cells were laid out in a line, it would span about 6 feet.

It's hard to imagine, but DNA molecules are so incredibly thin and long that if all the DNA in your body were laid out in a line, it would circle Earth more than two million times.

DNA molecules contain instructions for how to make a living thing. The instructions for assembling your body are like the instructions for assembling a robot. To build a robot, you must carefully follow an instruction manual to figure out how all the parts fit together.

But after following each step, your robot is assembled. Of course, your robot should have a name, just as you do. Maybe you've always liked the name Rusty.

Welcome to the world, Rusty!

DNA contains directions, just like Rusty's instruction manual does—but they're certainly not written with words on pages.

They're written with chemicals, which are the building blocks of every substance.

A DNA molecule looks like a long, twisted ladder, with rungs connecting the two sides. Scientists call this shape a double helix.

Four chemicals, which make up the rungs, are repeated over and over on the DNA ladder. The four chemicals are adenine, thymine, guanine, and cytosine. Scientists refer to them by their first letters: *A, T, G,* and *C.*

These chemicals can bond, or join together—but *A* can only bond with *T*, and *C* can only bond with *G*. When they bond, they are called base pairs. Base pairs are like the words in Rusty's assembly instructions, giving directions to cells for making protein molecules.

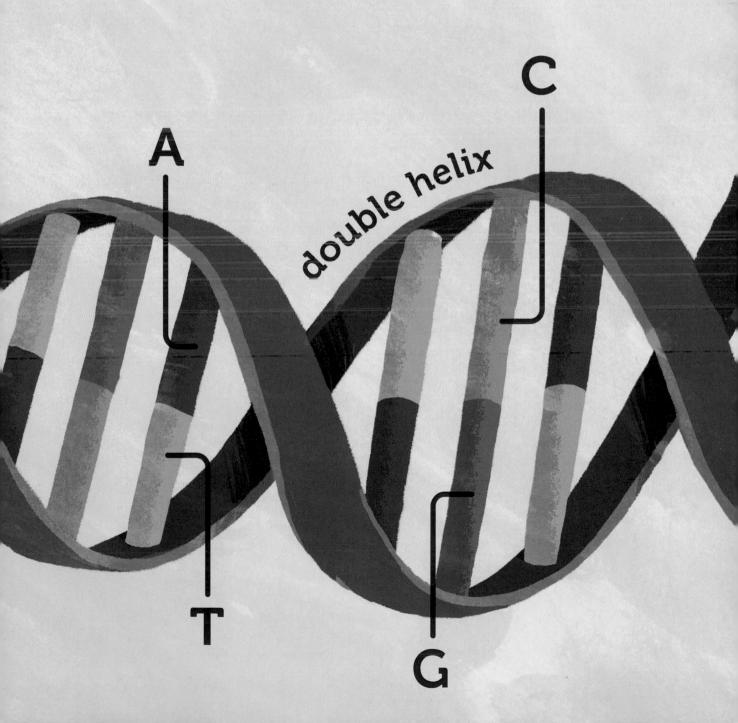

A

C

double helix

T

G

There are thousands of different kinds of protein molecules, which come in many different shapes and make up all the parts of your body.

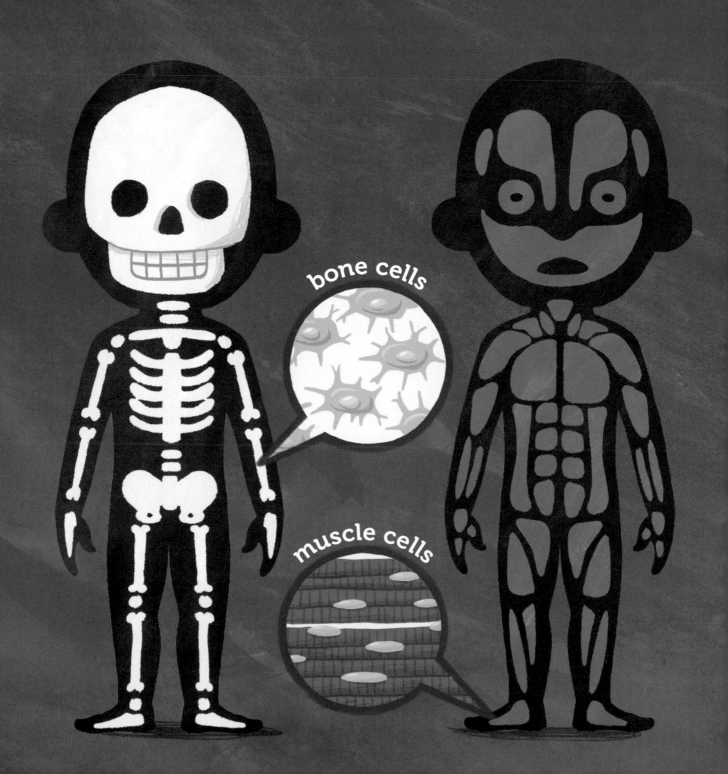

Proteins make up a big part of every living thing. Some protein molecules have the right shape to make your skin. Others make your bones or your muscles or your blood.

skin cells

blood cells

Your DNA not only directs the assembly of all your different body parts, but it also gives the directions for their exact locations in your body.

SKIN

skin cell

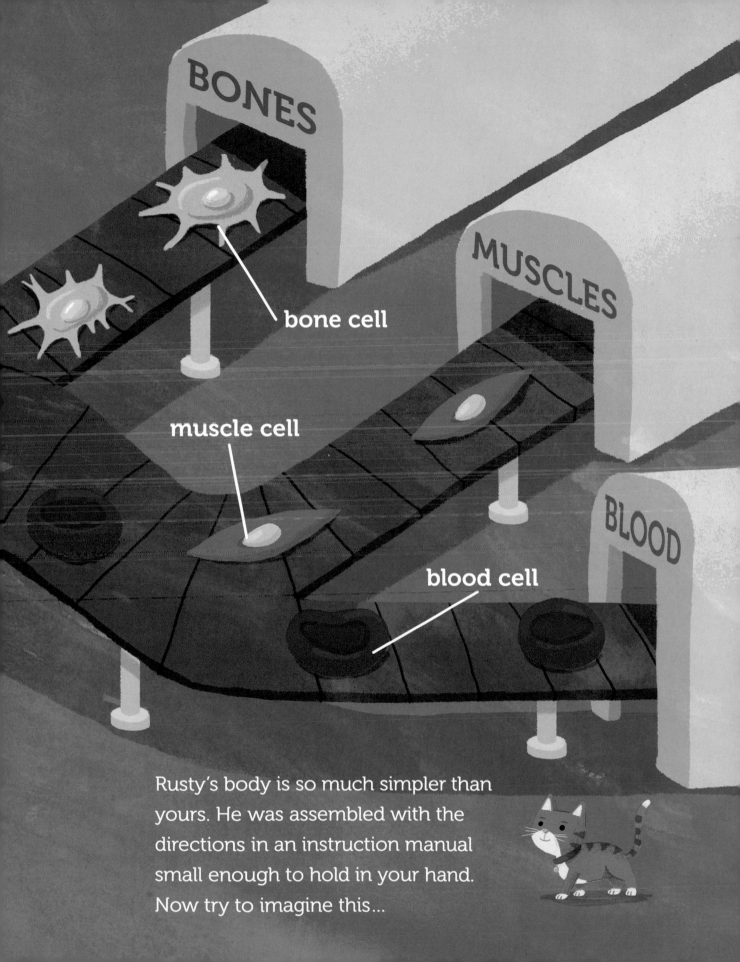

BONES

bone cell

MUSCLES

muscle cell

BLOOD

blood cell

Rusty's body is so much simpler than yours. He was assembled with the directions in an instruction manual small enough to hold in your hand. Now try to imagine this...

If the chemical directions for assembling you were written out on paper, like they are for a robot, they would fill two hundred very large instruction books, each with one thousand pages!

But once your body follows all the directions
in your DNA, you are a human being.

But why are you you, and not your brother or your neighbor?

The information in your cells' DNA is divided into smaller sections called chromosomes. Almost all human cells contain forty-six chromosomes, and they're each tightly wrapped up like thread on a spool. These tightly wrapped bundles make it possible to fit all six feet of a cell's DNA into the cell's nucleus.

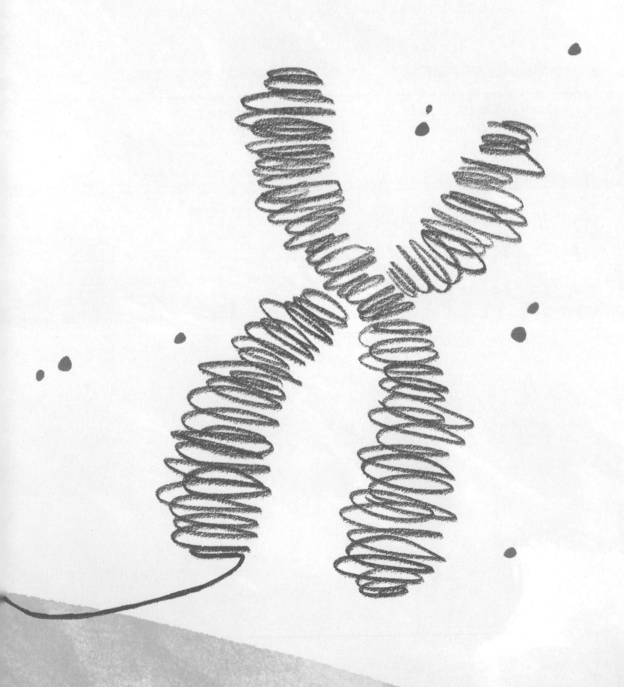

Each chromosome is divided again into smaller units called genes. Your body contains many thousands of genes.

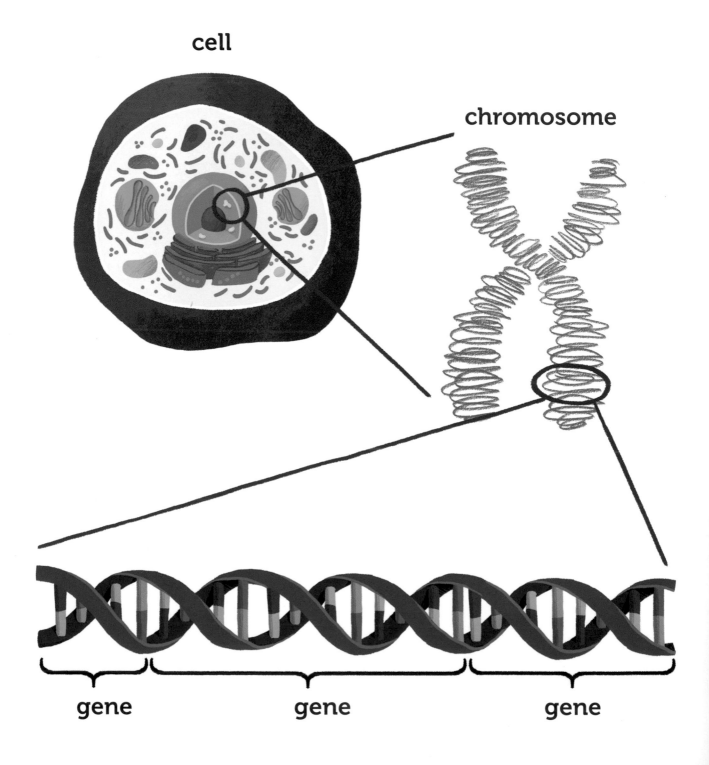

cell

chromosome

gene   gene   gene

No two people have exactly the same genes—
not even identical twins. Identical twins start
in the womb with identical genes, but slight
changes occur before they're born.

The instructions in your genes determine many of your individual features, including the shape of your nose, the size of your feet, or the color of your hair. They can even determine the sound of your laugh.

Your cells contain twenty-three chromosomes from your biological father and twenty-three from your biological mother. So, you get half of your genes from each parent. That's why you might have a nose like your dad and eyes like your mom.

There are billions of people on planet Earth, and in many ways they all are a lot alike. In fact, everyone's DNA molecules are more than 99 percent the same. That is what makes us all human beings.

But there are differences between each person too. Some people are short; some are tall. Some people have straight hair; some have curly hair. This is because of the fraction of a percent difference between each person's DNA.

That small variation in your DNA is part of what makes you one of a kind—and you can be proud of that!

Glossary

biological: related to life and living things

cell: the smallest structure in a living thing that can function by itself

chemical: something that cannot be broken up without changing into something else

chromosome: a section of DNA that specifies traits in a living thing

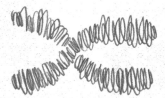

DNA: deoxyribonucleic acid; material that controls inherited traits in living things

gene: a single unit that defines inherited traits, made up of DNA and contained within each chromosome

identical: the same

microscope: a tool designed to make small objects appear bigger

molecule: the smallest part of a substance that has all the traits of that substance

nucleus: the central body of a cell

protein: an organic molecule within living things

Selected Sources

Begley, Sharon. "Decoding the Human Body." *Newsweek*, April 10, 2000.

Cevallos, Marissa. "Alphabet of Life." *Science News*, February 12, 2011: 18–21.

Gibbs, Nancy. "The Secret of Life." *Time*, February 17, 2003.

Gribbin, John, ed. *A Brief History of Science*. Lewes, England: The Ivy Press, 1998.

How the Body Works. New York: DK, 2016.

Lemonick, Michael D. "A Twist of Fate." *Time*, February 17, 2003.

Poole, Robert M., ed. *The Incredible Machine*. Washington, DC: National Geographic Society, 1986.

Ridley, Matt. "What Makes You Who You Are." *Time*, June 2, 2003.

Watson, James D. *DNA: The Secret of Life*. New York: Alfred A. Knopf, 2003.